What a Wonderful World

Feeling Good To Live In This World

You Always Have Other Options
Which one will you choose?

Written by
Janine Fletcher

Book illustrations by

....

(Write your own name here)
Where you see a picture frame, draw a picture about what you've just read.

DISCLAIMER

The suggestions in this book for personal growth are not meant to substitute for the advice of a trained professional such as a medical doctor, psychologist, therapist etc. It is essential to consult such a professional in the case of any physical or mental symptoms.

What A Wonderful World

YAHOO Feel Good Series

Being Your Own Best Friend
(Feeling Good To Be Me)

Feeling Good On The Inside
(Feeling Good To Be Alive)

What A Wonderful World
(Feeling Good To Live In This World)

(Feeling Good To Be Alive)

What A Wonderful World
(Feeling Good To Live In This World)

Welcome to planet earth.

Just for a little while I want you to imagine that this is the first time you have ever been to planet earth; to look at the world you live in with fresh eyes.

Take a look around you.

You look at the sky and you notice how it just goes on forever, it never seems to end. You take a deep breath and you can feel how endless it feels to be the sky. You say "Thank you" to the sky and this makes you feel even more endless.

Where you see a picture frame, draw a picture about what you've just read.

You see how the clouds seem to just float in the air. You take a deep breath and you can feel what it feels like to float in the air. You say "Thank you" to the clouds and this makes you float even more.

You see a flock of birds flying and you notice the lightness and ease of the way they fly. You take a deep breath and you can feel how free and light it feels to be a bird. You say "Thank you" to the birds and this makes you feel even more free and light.

You lie down on the grass and notice how soft and cool it feels. You take a deep breath and you can feel how fresh and alive it feels to be the grass. You say "Thank you" to the grass and this makes you feel even more fresh and alive.

You go for a swim in the ocean and you can't believe how exciting it is to let the waves take you for a ride. You take a deep breath and you can feel how it feels to go with the flow of the waves.   You say "Thank you" to the ocean and this makes you feel even more what it feels like to 'go with the flow'.

You go to the top of a snow-covered mountain peak and you notice how small everything looks from the top of the mountain. You take a deep breath and you can feel how strong and safe it feels to be the mountain. You say "Thank you" to the mountain and this makes you feel even more strong and safe.

You see some flowers and you are amazed at how beautiful and different each flower is. You take a deep breath and you can feel how beautiful and special it feels to be a flower. You say "Thank you" to the flowers and this makes you feel even more beautiful and unique.

You look up at the night sky and all of the stars. You take a deep breath and you can feel what it feels like to shine so brightly. You say "Thank you" to the stars and this makes you shine even more brightly.

You see rivers, jungles, waterfalls, trees, lions, tigers, elephants ...
You see all of this and much, much more.

You feel the strength, the beauty, the freedom, the freshness, the aliveness...
You feel all of this and much, much more.

"Wow!" You say to yourself, "What a wonderful world this is."

You hear some squeals of excitement, loud cheering and lots of laughter somewhere so you go to investigate.

You find people playing games like football, soccer, baseball, hockey, basketball, netball, tennis, bowls, and cricket. You take a deep breath and you can feel the sense of belonging and cooperation that people feel when they are part of a team.

You find people running, jumping, climbing, skipping, hopping, jogging, dancing, and doing yoga. You take a deep breath and you can feel how energetic and alive you feel when you exercise your body.

You find people reading, writing, drawing, painting, acting, singing, playing instruments and performing. You take a deep breath and you can feel the joy of creating and doing what you love.

You find people riding on boats, trains, buses, cars, aeroplanes, horses, canoes, jet skis, motorbikes, bicycles, scooters, skate boards, and hot air balloons. You take a deep breath and you can feel the excitement and freedom of being able to travel the world.

You find people skiing down snowy mountains, skating on ice, surfing, swimming, snorkeling, diving, parachuting, boogey-boarding, and much, much more.

You see people making sandcastles, playing chasey, playing hide-and-seek, playing on swings, sliding down slides, going on Ferris wheels and roller coasters and much, much more.

You see people going to zoos, museums, art galleries, national parks, concerts, theme parks, movies and much, much more.

"Wow!" You say to yourself, "So many fun things to do. It really is a wonderful world".

At one of the theme parks you see a person with an ice-cream and you think to yourself, "I would really like an ice-cream now too", so you buy one.

It is the best ice cream you have ever, ever tasted.

It tastes so good you want to say thank you to the person who made it and tell them how good it is.

You make your way back to the lady who served you at the ice-cream stall. She tells you she didn't make the ice cream… but she did serve you, so you thank her anyway.

You start to think ...Isn't it great that the ice-cream is so cold and,

You think some more...

Maybe I should thank the person who put the ice-cream in the fridge too.

And, you think some more...

Maybe I should thank all of the people who helped to make the fridge.

And, you think some more...

Maybe I should thank the truck driver for delivering the ice cream to the ice-cream stall.

And, you think some more...

Maybe I should thank the man at the petrol station for putting petrol in the delivery truck.

And, you think some more...

Maybe I should thank the farmer for milking the cows to get the milk, to help make the ice-cream.

And, you think some more...

Maybe I should thank the person who made up the recipe for the best ice-cream I have ever tasted.

And, you think some more...

So many people to thank and that is just for one of the best ice-creams I have ever tasted.

All of this thinking has made you hungry so you make your way to the food stall and buy a salad sandwich.

You find a shady tree and you sit down to eat your sandwich.

It is the best salad sandwich you have ever, ever tasted.

It tastes so good you want to say thank you to the person who made it and tell them how good it is.

You make your way back to the man who served you at the food stall. He tells you he didn't make the sandwich... but he did serve you, so you thank him anyway.

You start to think …Isn't it great that the bread is so fresh.
And, you think some more…
Maybe I should thank the person who made the bread too.

And, you think some more…
Maybe I should thank all of the people who helped to make the oven that the bread was baked in.

And, you think some more…
Maybe I should thank the farmers for growing the lettuce, the tomato, the cucumber, the beetroot and the carrot.

And, you think some more…
Maybe I should thank the truck drivers for taking the lettuce, the tomato, the cucumber, the beetroot and the carrot to the fruit and vegetable shop.

And you think some more…
Maybe I should thank the service station owners for selling petrol for the trucks that the truck drivers drive.

And you think some more…
Maybe I should thank all of the people who helped to make the trucks that the truck drivers drive.

And, you think some more…
Maybe I should thank the people who helped to build the shops to sell the fruit and vegetables.

And, you think some more...
Maybe I should thank the people in the fruit and vegetable shops for selling the lettuce, the tomato, the cucumber, the beetroot and the carrot.

And you think some more...

So many people to thank and that is just for one of the best salad sandwiches I have ever tasted.

All of this thinking has made you thirsty so you make your way to the drink stall and buy a drink. You sit back under the shady tree to drink your drink.

It is the best drink you have ever, ever tasted.

It tastes so good you want to say thank you to the person who made it and tell them how good it is.

You make your way back to the lady who served you at the drink stall. She tells you she didn't make the drink... but she did serve you, so you thank her anyway.

You start to think …Isn't it great that the drink is so cold and fizzy.

And, you think some more…and you think some more…and you think some more…

Wow, wow, wow. What an amazing thing so many people working together.

"Wow!" You say to yourself, "So many people co-operating. It sure feels good to live in this world".

And you think some more… you think of all the things you have seen today, the buildings, the toys, the cars, buses, aero planes, roller coasters, canoes, skis, footballs, boats, fishing rods, books, chairs, tables, museums, parks, parachutes, scooters, skateboards, telephones, computers, motorbikes, trains, slides, swings…all of this and so much more. Hundreds, thousands, millions of people working together for every single thing you've seen today.

Thinking of all the things you've seen makes you feel happy inside. You take a deep breath and you smile.

A little boy walks past you and he smiles back at you. You notice how the smile makes him light up.

He passes the smile on to his mum. You notice how the smile makes her light up too.

A group of three girls walk past you and you're still smiling. One of the girls smiles back at you. You notice how her smile makes her light up.

She passes the smile on to both of her friends. You notice how their smiles make both of them light up too.

One by one you notice that all of the people start to light up when they smile and then they pass the smile on.

You can't stop smiling. You're more amazed than ever at how easy it is to light people up.
You start thinking, if this keeps spreading soon everyone will light up.

It's like a game, seeing how many people you can light up.

"Wow!" You say to yourself, "So many people smiling. It sure feels good to live in this world".

You're having so much fun...until you smile at a lady and she doesn't smile back. Her smile is up-side down. It's like she's turned her light off!

You notice that as people look at her their smiles turn up-side-down too. She's turning off everyone's lights!

You don't understand why she is doing this so you run after her to help her to turn her light back on.

When you finally catch up with her you ask her why her smile is up-side-down. She says she is sad and she just doesn't feel good.

You can hardly believe what you are hearing. "You live in this wonderful world and you don't feel good?" you ask.

The sad lady doesn't answer. She just looks down at the ground with her smile upside down and her light turned off.

You think to yourself, I wonder why she doesn't feel good. Why doesn't she see all of the amazing things that I've seen on planet earth?

Then you notice that her eyes are always looking down. That's why she can't see what's right in front of her!

You take the sad lady by the hand, and you tell her to...

Look up at the sky and notice how it just goes on forever, it never seems to end. You tell her to take a deep breath and feel how enormous it feels to be the sky.

You tell her to lie down on the grass and notice how soft and cool it feels. You tell her to take a deep breath and feel how fresh it feels to be the grass.

You tell her to look up at the sky again and see how the clouds can make themselves into different shapes. You tell her to take a deep breath and feel the fun and the playfulness the clouds feel when they make themselves into many different shapes.

You tell her all of these things and so much more.

"Wow! What a wonderful world this is," the sad lady says to you.
You notice that her smile is not so up-side-down anymore and that her light is slowly turning on.

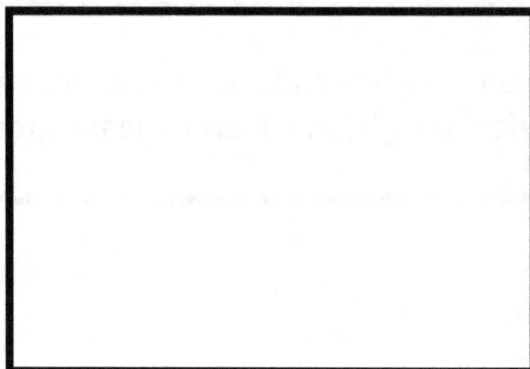

"Listen", you say to the sad lady, and she hears the squeals of excitement, loud cheering and lots of laughter coming from somewhere. "Let's go and investigate', the sad lady says excitedly.

She finds people playing games like football, soccer, baseball, hockey, basketball, netball, tennis, bowls, cricket, and so much more.

She finds people running, jumping, climbing, skipping, hopping, jogging, fishing, dancing, doing yoga and so much more.

She finds people reading, writing, drawing, painting, acting, singing, playing instruments, performing and so much more.

You show the sad lady all of the things you had found before. You show her all of these things and so much more.

"Wow!" the sad lady says to you, "So many fun things to do."
 You notice that she is almost smiling now and that her light is coming on.

At one of the theme parks the sad lady sees a person with an ice-cream and she says, 'I would really like an ice-cream now too', so you buy her one.

"Thank you, for buying me the ice-cream", she says to you.

You both sit under the shady tree while the sad lady eats her ice-cream.

It is the best ice cream she has ever, ever tasted.

It tastes so good she wants to say thank you to the person who made it and tell them how good it is.

She makes her way back to the lady who served you at the ice-cream stall. She tells her she didn't make the ice cream… but she did serve you, so she thanks her anyway.

The sad lady says to you,"Isn't it great that the ice-cream is so cold?
Maybe I should thank the person who put the ice-cream in the fridge too."

Then she says,
"Maybe I should thank all of the people who helped to make the fridge."

Then she says,
"Maybe I should thank the truck driver for delivering the ice cream to the ice-cream stall."

Then she says,
"Maybe I should thank the man at the petrol station for putting petrol in the delivery truck."

She says all of this and so much more.

"So many people to thank," she says, "and that is just for one of the best ice-creams I have ever tasted."

The sad lady talks about of all the things you have seen today; the buildings, the toys, the cars, buses, aero planes, roller coasters, canoes, skis, footballs, boats, fishing rods, books, chairs, tables, museums, parks, parachutes, scooters, skateboards, telephones, computers, motorbikes, trains, slides, swings...all of this and so much more.

"Wow, wow, wow!" the sad lady says, "Hundreds, thousands, millions of people working together for every single thing we've seen today. What an amazing thing to see so many people working together. What a wonderful world we live in."

The sad lady takes a deep breath and smiles a smile so big it lights up her whole face!

A little boy walks past and he smiles back at her. "Did you notice how his smile makes him light up?" she asks you.

"Mmm", you answer with a smile bigger than ever on your face.

One by one you notice that all of the people start to light up again,
and you think' to yourself," It sure feels **great** to live in this wonderful world!"

Remember to feel good to live in this world...

TAKE A LOOK AROUND YOU

What do you see?

Take a deep breath and feel what it feels like to be what you see.

SAY THANK YOU

Think about all of the people you would like to thank for some of your favourite things.

Count as many as you can.

Can you think of 10, 20, 100!?

SMILE

Put a smile on your face and pass it on.

How many people can you light up?

Information for Parents and Teachers

The **Yahoo series of 'Feel Good'** books are designed to work at the most fundamental level of how we are neurologically wired; the structure of the human brain.

The neural connections in our brain are formed by repetition and reinforcement. Learning to walk, talk, ride a bike, drive a car, read, write and so on are examples we can easily identify with to understand how we learn to do something.

The more we practise and reinforce any skills, the more automatic they become. When it becomes automatic for us, we no longer have to be conscious of what we're doing, we're just doing it.

Having a positive attitude and learning to feel good about ourselves can be understood in a similar way. As we repeat thoughts, emotions and actions over and over again, they become automatic patterns of behaviour; the way our brain is wired up.

What we may fail to understand is that the brain doesn't discriminate among thoughts on the neurological level. It takes no more effort to form a positive thought than it does a negative one. Attitudes are simply accumulations of related neural nets and positive attitudes are just as easy to construct as negative ones. (Evolve Your Brain By Joe Dispenza p.449).

Over time, by applying and practising the concepts presented in the 'Yahoo Feel Good' series of books this way of thinking will become the dominant/automatic way of thinking, feeling and acting because it's the way the brain has been wired.

It is recommended that your child illustrate the pages in this book. As your child is thinking about how to illustrate the concepts presented in the text, it will help stimulate and establish positive neural connections. Each time the story is re read or the concepts discussed, these connections will be activated and reinforced.

With consistent awareness, repetition and reinforcement, these thoughts will become beliefs; embedded in the child's neurology; the structure of their brain.

www.ingramcontent.com/pod-product-compliance
Lightning Source LLC
LaVergne TN
LVHW061341060426
835511LV00014B/2061